DATA MIND

Also by Joanna Fuhrman

To a New Era

The Year of Yellow Butterflies

Pageant

Moraine

Ugh Ugh Ocean

Freud in Brooklyn

DATA MIND

POEMS

JOANNA FUHRMAN

Curbstone Books / Northwestern University Press
Evanston, Illinois

Curbstone Books
Northwestern University Press
www.nupress.northwestern.edu

Printed in the United States of America

10   9   8   7   6   5   4   3   2   1

Library of Congress Cataloging-in-Publication Data

Names: Fuhrman, Joanna, 1972– author.
Title: Data mind : poems / Joanna Fuhrman.
Description: Evanston, Illinois : Curbstone Books/Northwestern University Press,
    2024.
Identifiers: LCCN 2024021393 | ISBN 9780810147744 (paperback) |
    ISBN 9780810147751 (ebook)
Subjects: LCSH: American poetry—21st century.
Classification: LCC PS3556.U3247 D38 2024 | DDC 811/.54—dc23/
    eng/20240516
LC record available at https://lccn.loc.gov/2024021393

Experience is a hoax.

—Alice Notley

CONTENTS

DATA MIND

I wanted everyone to feel the way my teeth vibrated, but when I posted my glow-in-the-dark selfie only the closet mermaids noticed. I didn't blame anyone. I knew the oceans were walking heavy-footed on the land. It was one of those afternoons when I was sure that God was the series of tubes connecting my brain to the torso of a deer. Was it possible that the self was larger than the country that birthed it? Could a mouth open large enough to accommodate the girth of a bloated nation's whale? I hung a sign that read "Hope" on the taxidermied body of an owl and waited for applause. Children gathered around to worship, sticking microchips and slivers of sunlight in its missing, blinking eye.

ARE YOU THE INVISIBLE SONG THAT WAS PLAYING?

To wear a blindfold in the algorithmic state one must trust that the crowd is closer to a mosh pit than an ocean. One morning your glass of orange juice is replaced by a beacon of sunlight and from then on the square of sadness you carry in your pocket feels heavier.

When I was a data point, I posted to a forum a question about the effects of perimenopause, and when the answers came back, I trembled in their presence. My love of the internet was like my love of the city. In each, I wandered underground, smelling of pomegranates and hemorrhoid cream.

Yesterday, on the subway, I overheard a woman with a voice like a cartoon parrot complaining of her Macy's coworker's purchase of a thong for clubbing, "The picture showed just what it is—a sack for your dick and balls."

so no one can see your red pimple or your purple wheelchair. My optimism about this is stuck in 1997, but what do you expect from a woman whose wrinkles are deep enough to reach her subconscious?

As a preteen, when I first rode the subway alone, I carried a heavy Walkman, listening to upbeat songs about the end of the world. Back then, the cars were wrapped in unreadable, brightly colored names.

I thought of poetry as a way to get lost like the internet, but I hadn't yet heard of the internet.

Back then, I didn't need to get lost to feel lost.

I spent so many hours on the phone talking to my friends that my neck ached.

I wrote in a poem, "Talking is like going swimming in a small pool. You think it's the ocean until you bang into the rail."

I baked a cake in the shape of a moon, and no one could tell what was a cake and what was the moon. When I cut it open, it tasted like overly sweetened watermelon tea and smelled like the shadow of the leaves on a lake. I loved it, but then the bloggers arrived complaining that my baking was "bougie." So I crafted a cake in the shape of my face. It had curly hair, glasses, and an open mouth that could keep talking even when no one was listening. In my big marble-cake nose, I hid my people's struggles, the escape from the pogroms and the years of overly salty chicken. I loved that cake too but was ashamed to admit it. I had read that identity politics was just the cream filling of neoliberalism. So I baked a cake that was messy like New York. I cut it open and rode the subways inside, eating my way through dirty, glistening sidewalks like a hungry Frank O'Hara. But that was the year everyone claimed to be Frank O'Hara—even those numskulls who hated Modern Art. So I baked a cake shaped like the internet, and when I cut it open, everyone who tasted it said it tasted just like the internet, and I kept eating it and eating it and eating it, in a kind of durational performance, until the cake itself was the internet and I myself the somewhat delicious crumbs.

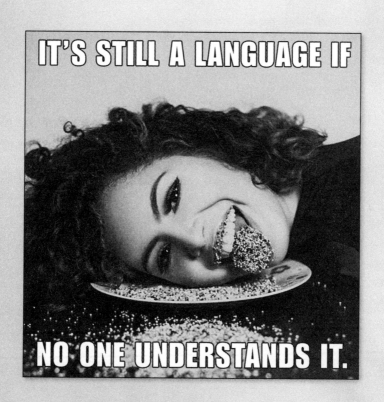

IF A MENOPAUSAL WOMAN DANCES IN A JUNGLE AND NOBODY FILMS IT

A child in Belize dances like a banana peel on a yellow afternoon.

An old woman with a face like a banana peel performs the same dance in the middle of a riot.

I open my laptop and hear a million voices speaking to me at once. Is this how Santa Claus feels when the world's murmuring desires continually interrupt his Wordle?

As the child dances, other children mirror his moves. Left hand to the sky, right leg toward the disappearing ocean.

When one of the dancing arms crashes through the screen, becoming a barking Dogecoin, another arm morphs into jazz.

The old woman is thinking about the protests she got lost in as a teen, the way the air smelled of flat beer, how once, in the middle of a crowd, she overheard a couple break up. Afterward the man and woman had to stay together: the chanting protesters confined their bodies to the movement of the swarm.

Now all the children dance as if they were one child.

A dog watching on an iPad in Tampa tries to mimic the moves, but looks like a malfunctioning robot horse. A lawyer in Edgewood does every move one step behind with more booty. A baker in Belfast jerks along, his bell-covered hip scarf awkwardly bouncing off spandex leggings.

Now the orange kitchen in Belize is revealed to be the top of a skyscraper in Singapore. The old woman who claimed she was remembering the friend she made at the Selma bus boycott is not an old woman. A Chihuahua in a salt-and-pepper wig, she stars in a streaming ad for squeezable cheese.

Still, when Lizzo pops up, her skin shimmering like an inside-out ocean, the computer screen hiccups birds. I read a poem on my iPad and the pixels break into Cheez-Its.

A banana peel dances. A banana peel is always dancing somewhere.

The child opens his chest. If twenty other children fly out, he knows he's ready to begin.

DID YOU KNOW THAT YOUR DOPPELGÄNGER IS LICKING CHAOS ON THE DARK WEB?

She's crafting Purim cakes out of the blowtorched carcasses of last Thanksgiving's turkeys, leading glow-up tutorials for itinerant mushroom clouds, gaining a following for her ASMR-inspired parenting technique, redecorating her mudroom using only syringes from defunded needle exchange programs. And yes, even if she failed to build a following for her hairshirt competitive-Piloxing tournament, and her sext to her daughter's college prof got leaked then turned into memes, you can't minimize her success lipreading the habits of highly successful crustaceans, or ignore the admiration she earned after she—from the mouth of a live volcano—livestreamed giving birth to a dragon. When she traded her red handkerchief for the screech of a hawk, the chips on the table caught fire. Have you ever considered that it's your hair that's burning? If so, please click here. A refund is on the way.

YOU WON'T BELIEVE HOW YOUR FAVORITE CHILDHOOD STAR LOOKS NOW

Your favorite childhood star sports a fuchsia goatee, an extra arm named Felix, and a Hamburglar-shaped red cheek piercing. He once adopted a pet nation-state, but he had to give it back when his life coach became allergic. No one knows who he is because his sunglasses are made of cracked cell phone screens. He knows who everyone is because he invested in yeti tech. If you were to spend your Sunday with him, you'd discover how much he enjoys lounging on his Kimberly Guilfoyle–brand overstuffed settee, brunch with his ex, and a walk around what used to be a soup factory but is now a luau-themed coworking space. Despite a difficult decade where his heart was said to occasionally stop for forty-five to sixty-nine seconds, he has chosen to embrace the sunny side of the empty glass. Like many child stars, he is most happy when he's asleep, clutching a stuffie with a face custom printed to resemble you, his most loyal fan.

PREQUEL

When their offspring is revealed to be a motherboard, the parents add two eye-shaped cameras on what will come to be referred to as a face. On its first birthday, the guests' demographics are stirred into a baby-shaped cake. They smile for snapshots, later published on the baby's skin. In school, its measurements are posted and reposted on a spaceship's bulletin board, its grades projected on the sky. For graduation, a number is added to its nomenclature. At its first job, a Geiger counter is strapped to its bank account, its thoughts repackaged as knickknacks for a museum's gift shop or chopped apart to feed the burgeoning minivans. Years later, at the combination wedding/funeral, the celebrants and mourners open their wallets to find the former infant's smile inscribed on currency, images of the circuits edited into their porn.

rips pages out of spell books and mixes them with Diet Coke. She sprays her innards with stray rumors, so her heart cavities smell like red Jolly Ranchers. She replaces your pocket mirror with snapshots of the cool people you envy.

When she wears her silk pajamas inside out, the seams get stuck on the furniture. When she gives a lecture on loss, all the Barbies tear off their own heads. Replace their missing skulls with bejeweled pocketknives.

Did you know she started out as a canine copy of your soul? She would wear your face on her fur, and when you slept it would turn into the visage of the popular girl you wanted to be. Celestial eyelashes. A frying pan for a mouth.

As a teenage werewolf, she slept at the top of a flickering lighthouse and howled at your crayon drawing of the moon. As an elderly Sasquatch, she mocked your earnest attempt at a tweet.

THE YEAR THE INTERNET WAS A
GLITCHING MAP

To the West, an ocean of hand sanitizer convulsing in waves, a mountain of rhinestones plucked from the foreheads of dead flaneurs.

To the East, holograms of the Bee Gees wiggling in sequined masks. An American flag wrapping itself around a vat of bleeding meat. A neon sign flickering *untranslatable*.

To the South, a flashlight that shines on an open palm revealing the future of the president everyone should hate. A marshmallow shaped like a finger jamming the hole in a busted dam. A baby in work boots digging a hole. Another baby hoarding diapers in preparation for a rumored war.

To the North, a valentine covering the face of the Confederate general. A kombucha river scented with whiskey and wine.

At the center is me: an empty bottle of honking. A compass rose in the shape of a fist.

Like a barbecued eel on a sushi plate, like the whir of a rowboat over static, everything in her life was software. In an empty chatroom in 1993, she found a stranger's glow-in-the-dark brain wiggling and saw her own brain plummeting from above. Soon it felt like everything was happening on the same pin tip. She gave up cigarettes, novels, needlework, doodling, Diet Coke, and all her AFK friends. She thought, *Why not just try some mac-and-cheese pastrami pie with groundhog foam for a chaser?* Why not change your name and shoe size, move in with a gray-bearded stranger and his collection of ex-girlfriends and owl mugs? You might as well drop out, might as well dress up your avatar in smashed Erector sets and scars.

IT'S NOT A LANGUAGE IF EVERYONE UNDERSTANDS IT

The problem with living one's life online is that there is no problem. You wake up, pet the cat, throw some words into the void, and the next thing you know your death is sitting right there, wearing a red prom gown and throwing paper airplanes through the window. Is this what you imagined it would smell like when your childhood unraveled? Burnt rose stems? Underwire bras? The night you dream about getting fitted for a wet suit, your teeth grow three centimeters. The station wagon buried in the backyard comes to life, demanding open-faced sandwiches and overpriced psychoanalysis. Your mother wakes up in her grave and wants to know why you are storing sanitary napkins in her favorite yellow purse. *It's not a language if no one understands it,* you want to scream at your lawn gnome, but you don't own a lawn gnome. Yesterday, you tried lining up all of your favorite words in a row as if you were a sous chef, as if God would come around later, combine them into some sort of meal.

HOW IT STARTED / HOW IT'S GOING

I was reading a blog, trying to find a recipe for lentil stew, but the story about the writer's stepdaughter's missing slipper went on for so long that by the time I arrived at the ingredient list the building our apartment is in had been sold and resold and sold again, and even worse our kitchen had been replaced with a digital oven that turned all ingredients into different flavors of miniature muffins: tofu piccata muffins, charcoal fondue muffins, hillbilly elegy muffins, death metal NFT muffins, raspberry nepo-baby marble dildo muffins. One day, I threw a muffin at the moon, and—to my surprise—the moon threw a muffin back. I told everyone in my activist Slack feed that this was a new kind of radical action, made more potent by its engagement in celestial intersectionality. Soon we were a whole movement of revolutionary bakers, a federation of militant muffin throwers designed to augment anti-capitalist baking with celestial praxis. Who could have known the muffins had other plans?

THESE SIX EMOJIS EXPLAIN YOUR LIFE
RIGHT NOW

I know how to wrap myself in other people's mishugas. All morning I read about the woman from Louisiana who can't stop her son from hiding under the bed, a man in South Korea learning to fish in a hotel bathtub, a child across town who swallowed a whole marshmallow shaped like the Guggenheim. I take screenshots of these strangers' problems and blend them into a banana-kale smoothie, drink it from a wineglass with my naked ass deeply sunk in a silk pillow. Afterward, my body is a pink cloud with winged sneakers. I hover above the data, rain down gossip on other people's pain. This is a kind of freedom, but also—what? A kind of tragic happiness like that cowboy who thinks he can lasso transcendence and tie it to his belt buckle. Or like that photo of the lake on fire your student posted as their Grindr pic, or at least claimed he did. Like everything else, you'll never actually know.

A HEART IS NOT A METAPHOR

Some afternoons I love the way the light spills from the sheet's eyehole, the way the scent from the neighbor's booty call illuminates the noise.

Some days it's enough to just unmake the bed, wreck the coffee by stirring in old tears, cover the TV with a scrim so all the characters resemble the good-looking zombies in an unknown Edward Hopper painting.

And yes, I know I can't erase the birthmark from my death certificate, can't remake my mouth into a permanent smile.

Still, the rumble beneath the mambo soothes me. Who wouldn't enjoy the elongated shadow a marred language leaves behind on the wall?

I asked ChatGPT to give me a metaphor for my childhood trauma, but it answered in a language only translatable by ghosts. When I Instant Messaged all the ghosts I knew, two of them were busy redecorating their goth/Barbiecore Airstream, one had gotten lost in a mega-market's new walk-in fridge, and the other three had taken hallucinogens made from rabbit poop and had yet to regain consciousness. So I opened my favorite coercive control exposé message board. This time, instead of the usual blog links and inside jokes, I saw a video of myself, and on it the scars from when I was ten and the substitute teacher hit me with an open bag of Funyuns. The screen was suddenly full of scars, not only my scars, but scars belonging to people I'd never met and scars on the flesh of people I had only met in the internet's speckled nonspace. All the scars. All scars. Wiggling scars. Popping and locking scars. Right there in the redacted comments of our subreddit: a chorus line of boogying scars cut the carpet into rugs. Years later—after I had gotten married, landed my dream job, bought a house, earned a title in my duckpin league, and learned to use the sous vide wand I had been given at my retirement party—I found that scar again. I had been examining my body in preparation for my annual dermatology appointment, and there it was. I had almost forgotten about it, but when I saw it again, I was not surprised to see it sway.

Data eats the edges off our temporary selves, and we emerge with our skin tags zapped, our missing leg hair a bridge between infanthood and now. Here, people work and sleep with their feet buried beneath expense reports and Nerf bananas. We plunder, jangle unfastened words, and yell *skedaddle* to the frog-masked ghosts. Money disappears and reappears as language, then glass. In the shadow cast by a giant clown nose, a crowd gathers to argue: *It's your fault if you don't like it that your gf wears her snorkel gear to happy hour. // You should admit that you accidentally ate your stepdaughter's marzipan frankfurter. // Fifty-three is too old to dress ironically like a grandma.* I crawl deeper into the rattling and build a nest out of strands of ticker tape and floss. Rainbow sprinkles cascade onto a cake made of *just* rainbow sprinkles. Teardrops morph into GIFs— crocodiles weeping in clawfoot tubs.

MY AMERICAN NAME IS MONEY

When you are a woman in the algorithmic state, everyone wants to taste your data, but you are unsure which of your limbs is data and which are twitching proofs of God.

You post online a cry for help. "Who if I cried out would see the me in the metadata?"

A cat in a sailor hat walks across the screen and it angers you that she looks nothing like your childhood pet.

Out the window in the alley, it's unclear if a roof is being fixed or destroyed. You wonder how much money have you lost on friendship. How much on the metaphysics of sky?

On your cell phone, there's a photo of a barbecued lamb shank. There's an emoji of a bright yellow face screaming in terror or joy.

PHOTOGRAPHING YOUR SALAD TURNS IT INTO A GHOST

Women who eat nothing but salad aren't really women, but figments of the culture's collective unconscious. One day one escapes the walls of the basement's television and bleeds her language all over the floor of the slaughterhouse. What did you expect? How many years could you spend eating iceberg lettuce and watching the shopping channel before you, too, would want to dress up as a 1975-era Patty Hearst and shoot fragments of the moon into the heart of the internet? Am I afraid to actually admit that this is just a story about the tiny mother who lives in my chest? Sometimes I catch her making a bed in my heart, polishing her gravy urn with patriarchy's spittle, and I want to surgically extract her with a nanobot. But then I remember how little I understand about place settings, so I accept her dated, meticulous ways. I open the liquor cabinet, watch her bathe in a lipstick-shaped glass.

WE'LL BURN THAT ALGORITHM WHEN WE GET TO IT

Smurfette is hiding in the binary code again, stirring up alphabet soup as if all that is needed to make meaning is some noodles in the shape of a word. She tells me all you need to resist being a product is to feel the spaces between the letters as they float together and apart.

I used to think this too. Now, I doubt this power.

I skip through profiles, admiring the fifth-wave cleavage of my post-Millennial pals, nostalgic for the burlap-sack feminism of my youth.

My husband is in the adjacent room, dismantling the surveillance cameras and using parts to build a statue of a god. I love him most like this—when all the windows are open, when all the computer eyes quiver and blink.

ME DAY!

If you don't have any family pictures to share, the internet will try to sell you eyeball grease. If you do, they'll try organic sunscreen and slogans. On Earth Day, I'm pitched a floral-scented battery, lemon verbena truffle salt, and a burnt-umber topological glossary. For Mother's Day, they try a quasi-real backbone. On Father's Day, a case of bro fragility and a double decker pin-up of a beetle.

On my birthday, I watch my memories sprout clown feet. I pickle my heart-shaped vegetarian liver in dill and pectin. Pick my pimple until its auguries spill out.

When the outline of the United States overlaps with my face on the screen, daylight becomes a mask without a language to break it. I fly backward into what I think is the past. Lost in the open lips of an advertisement, I kiss the shadow of an embarrassing crush.

DOES THIS DATA MAKE ME LOOK FAT?

I am hiding from the algorithm in a fossilized dinosaur egg. It's warm here but too moist, like a hotel room that smells of a previous guest's saliva. From inside, I can't hear the ghosts digging under the carpet or see the white glove as it slides off the photo of an old woman's hand.

My mother's voice is the only sound I hear, but she's speaking some ancestor's mother tongue that I can't understand. Her words sound like the color of smoke . . . the frequency of movie-theater red, the puckered mouths of hot-dog tails.

Years ago, I flew over the city in a helicopter, watched another version of myself on the street below. The other me was clicking on the screen of an oversized cell. I could tell that she had better teeth than I did. She was wittier, and her skin had fewer blotches. When I spoke, I longed for her voice to come flowing out of my mouth.

For almost an hour, I held my lips open, but only a breeze streamed out.

I was six years old when I entered the pink internet, and two hundred and three when I left. Inside the plastic dream school, I learned to modulate my organ noise so my body parts glowed in the dark. I covered my scars in silk whispers and strung paper carnations where I thought better body parts should be. Behind the plush blackboard, meringue-covered spaceships ate my body hair and spit it out as data. My body kept replicating itself until the walls of the classroom and the bodies were one. I tried so hard to figure out what I wanted that by the time I figured out what I wanted, the view from the window had changed. The jungle gym was replaced with projected images of actual jungles. There were real monkeys swinging from filmed images of trees. Some days I was convinced that I was a monkey too, that it was me I saw out the window, it was me the whole class gawked at, me baring my big ass, me flaunting my fangs. That high-pitched squeal—that was mine too, it was me screeching—my voice piercing the building's walls.

BARBIE ATTEMPTS TO GAIN CONTROL OF THE ALGORITHMIC STATE

She was lucky that her fingers were small enough to fit into the microprocessor and pull out a rubber chicken. Raggedy Ann watched with envy. She'd been standing on the edge of the digital highway for forty-one days and forty-two nights and no one seemed to notice. Everyone was born knowing love is unfair, but the unfairness of rubber chickens surprised her. She felt angry at the future's reflection in her button eyes and tried to express it by adding extra chunks to the cookies. Barbie didn't catch the innuendo. The daytime moon followed her as she danced around her fuchsia bedroom. The microprocessor in her heels auto-tuned the bird's song. Her vintage Google glasses tinted the view of the dying hydrangea. Outside, a tidal wave of strangers tried to remake the narrative. They praised the way social media keeps you from obsessing on a single other. They formed a circle around a circle around a home where nothing used to be. "Blank doesn't mean nothing" read the words on the teeth of a god.

MY BREAST SQUIRTS MILK AT THE ALGORITHMIC STATE

I will never be a mother, but that doesn't mean this action is metaphoric. Liquid is always both tenor and vehicle, reality and dream. When we have sex, all the computers in the apartment fall asleep. The cell phone enters another dimension, slips between the cabinet's purple aura and the crack in the sky. Does this imply my teenage self is still here, wearing red panties to camouflage the blood? Like any other teenager, she is looking for a comfortable pause, a window with a strong enough rope. Like any other old hag, I am settling for a mug of hot cocoa, a sword-style letter opener, and a kiss.

At the three-minute-and-thirty-eight-second mark, the kitten transforms into 1984 Jane Fonda. She lifts her knee and behind her skinny thigh, Ronald Reagan's two-dimensional face rotates on the legs of a plastic windup toy. The distance between then and now is unsealed. A slightly shinier 1971 Jane Fonda uses her placard to swat flies, and a twenty-first-century Jane coiffed in a tweed Chanel blazer rolls her eyes. For a moment, all three women are one. For a moment, one Jane holds the other Janes in her palm. A single go-go boot sprouts wings. The toaster sticks out its tongue. All three Janes wear similar smiles in different shades of watermelon pink. All three Janes hold hands like Matisse's dancing ladies, sing in a language only the future will understand.

—

In the spaces between the women, reality undulates and flickers. It takes the edges off the objects and replaces them with hums. It skinny-dips in static. It tells you if you want to be believed, choose one or the other. Are you the good Jane or the bad? For one dollar and two cents, you can try on a Jane wig and be transformed into clamor. In *Barbarella*, all three Janes have sex with a frog who looks like the reader of this poem, but he is not the reader of this poem. There is no reader of this poem.

If you look closely at this space, you can see what will one day be called The Internet: a baby ghost in diapers licking the circumference between one realm and the next. If he leaves behind traces of his DNA, will a future forensics team sing his praises? Will he get credit for some crime none of us knew was taking place?

—

When The Internet is pristine like a basketball suspended in an all-white gallery, you can feel each organ in your body floating solidly in place. It feels like being made of marble. When The Internet is chaotic like one

Jane Fonda on two motorbikes, your limbs feel like you are swimming in an ocean of noise.

—

Your childhood hovers like a basketball in a lime-green Jell-O mold. Your childhood is both the lime-green Jell-O mold and the stainless-steel ball hovering within the beautiful shine.

At this moment, The Internet is born looking right at the lens to his audience in the next century.

When Jane Fonda was an infant, her teeth cut through time. This action created a forest, an electric river dividing the spaces between languages. It created the birth of The Internet as well as its eventual destruction.

No one is at fault for wanting to stay in this particular everywhere, for enjoying the cleansing mess of it. Who wouldn't enjoy the way language dissolves into sugar? Who wouldn't want to feel someone else's pulse within their skin—to be declared an official child, an offspring of panic and glass?

CLOSE ENCOUNTERS OF THE
TWENTY-FIRST KIND

When the cursor blinks, when it appears and disappears, do I, too, disappear? Do I collapse into another universe where the edges of sharp objects bleed into music? Is the feeling of falling into a beloved's arms forgotten, or have I just substituted one mode of sensation for another— the way connecting our brains with filaments replaced the landline? Or the way chatter replaces silence if one spends too much time alone? It's possible that each night when I put my sleep apnea mask on and unscrew the light bulbs from the fixtures, it's not the claws of the twentieth century I hear scurrying through the ceiling, but a future version of myself. Does this version still need weekly sex and poppyseed flagels with lox? Is she happy just being a sort of antimatter matter? A circle with a big nose strapped to it? A screen with a pair of Groucho mustache glasses? A pillow? If beds are more comfortable when repurposed as satellites circling the moon, when the aliens supersede us, will we mind? I've heard everyone's teeth look better surrounded by green.

I was not surprised to learn that the character of Smurfette in *The Matrix* was played by the Holy Trinity: her brain was God, her body Jesus, her weapons Holy Ghosts. The actual Smurfette is angry that in real life she never got to kick any digital asses. I tried to explain to her that in the current version of fifty-first-wave feminism, we hate violence, but her hands had already turned into boxing gloves. Despite my pleas, she swings them wildly into the binary code mustache of Burt Reynolds.

When I wake up, my mouth has been replaced with a centipede that crawls across the screen of my face. My husband has been replaced by a young Keanu Reeves who looks like he's remembering the thrill he felt when he first wrote his name in pee.

In my chest, a television is playing the movie's commercial break: an ad for imitation pheromones, starring the ghost of Ronald Reagan.

In the tunnels of the ad, those spaces between the pixels, a version of myself is dressed as a female Orpheus. Like always, I'm stuck looking back at that moment, perceiving both the lightning flash of the future and the dark everything of the past.

THE WARRIORS

I am rewriting the script to *The Warriors*.

In this version, our gang travels subterranean media drinking radioactive lite beer—or is it preverbal memories?

When they arrive at the boardwalk, the surveillance cameras flicker. Strangers battle each other with feathers or tweets.

After the hero takes off his clothes, he keeps removing parts of himself until all that's left is a heart-shaped gap where his brain used to be.

In the morning, the abandoned shopping mall is transformed into a hot-dog stand selling empty buns.

The zero at the heart of the narrative opens its mouth and swallows the plot. Two oceans become one. Five oceans become fifty-nine thousand bodies of water.

The wandering men become wandering mouths, then clicking fingers pretending to be free.

The computer transcribes the motorcycle's dreams and spits them out as broken glass, then data.

My childhood is dismantled and repacked as snacks.

What the audience remembers of the fight is just a series of dots and dashes.

What the fist remembers is the moment before the smack, that golden pocket of quiet.

What I remember of my script drips from the sky onto the glass keyboard.

What the crowd remembers is the journey below, what it's like to travel as a group—to see all the members as one body, then to watch it break apart.

In the remake of the film, Melanie Griffith's wig is made of a disassembled black Toyota. She doesn't drive anywhere. Instead, she makes love to a businessman in an abandoned diner bathroom, hoping that if they both grunt loud enough, the East Village of the '80s will return. For a moment it does—in front of the knish store on Houston, tangerine-scented meringue tickles the necks of amateur pickpockets. Ghosts with asymmetrical haircuts play three-card monte on the backs of runaway farm boys. When the current year snaps back, the bathroom mirror is splattered with blood. Curls from long-lost Nuyorican beauty salons clump together to create hair beasts, the future version of anti-capitalist pets. Neon data scrolls across a sunglasses' lens.

My hands in long white gloves slip through the monitor's watery screen, and I become the Princess of Death in Cocteau's *Orphée*. Are those my lungs floating or two fossilized Twinkies, salvaged from a previous millennium's deep ocean fridge? Time, a marble in a broken Rube Goldberg machine, wobbles, jerking both backward and forward. The ruins of a city fall inward and then back toward the dead. What sadness I harbored for the loss of the planet, I replace with a crying-face emoji. The anger I mean to direct at the oligarchs becomes the word **OLIGARCHS** (written in flashing Comic Sans). Orpheus, you claimed you were my companion in darkness, but it turns out you were just another so-called lyric peddler. Your face too symmetrical to be of use as a disorientation mechanism, your language too lovely to blow up the bank. I take off all my clothes, only to find more clothing replicating underneath.

CHAPSTICK TRACES

At the end of the movie, Ally Sheedy and Olivia Newton-John switch places. Their flesh pixilates. The blonde becomes a leather jacket and the brunette a pair of periwinkle flats. I travel back in time to help. We craft profiles for a new dating app popular among the newly dead. Soon, they've become one girl. Denuded. Skinny. Her skin ripples like low-hanging clouds. When she stares into a cell phone's lens, the ancient river where she was born flows into an ocean of data. Does this mean I have become her too, that my own lips leave ChapStick traces on the cave's motherboard wallpaper? Is it my own breath spiraling like a borrowed French kiss? Inside the algorithm, trees quiver like eyelashes. I slip off my blue jeans and replace them with calcified gossip. A fresh corpse mimics the poses of the newest pool-girl influencer. A message board becomes a featherless bird. When the bathroom mirror flickers with TikTok how-to videos, it's finally summer. The high school floats above, shedding bricks like flakes of old skin.

Gwyneth Paltrow cuts her hair. Dyes it blond to spite her cheating ex. In power suits, she hides her loneliness in the pocket square of the first Monty Python fan who mansplains crypto to her. The other Gwyneth, creature of cottage cheese canned-fruit salad, stays in the analog, gives her money to a boyfriend with a stutter, braids her hair into the window blind's cord. But where is the Gwyneth who can inhabit both Gwyneths? The crying-in-the-bathtub Gwyneth who drinks Manischewitz from a crystal vase while simultaneously gliding in an evening gown across an awestruck carpet of chandelier-kissed cater waiters? Can there be a Gwyneth inside each Gwyneth? An infinite regress of Gwyneths! If you stare at the corner of my cell's smashed screen, you can see their reflections, legible despite the surface's cracks. Here's the windup troll doll Gwyneth, the Gwyneth with librarian glasses and leather pants, the Gwyneth soaked in glistening placenta, the nose-bleed shamanic Gwyneth, the Gwyneth with a house-sized shovel, the Gwyneth running, flying a kite shaped like her own face.

IN *THE MATRIX* STARRING NICOLAS CAGE

Neo is a piss-ass drunk, and it doesn't matter if alcohol is only an idea. Meaning detaches from language and flies in slow motion like shampoo-commercial hair. The absent women shift behind the curtains, a mother's face camouflaged by a William Morris floral, a sister's breath hidden by the smell of an off-season fireplace. The twenty-first century is riding a bloodshot Ferrari into the mouth of climate change, and it needs pure vodka to make it okay. Nic is naked all the time. Even naked, he sweats through his clothes. Even when he's fully dressed, his dick swings unsheathed. *You* try lassoing the sky's panopticon with only a goddamned body part. He knows the world isn't real, so why not just buy a big-ass blowup doll? Why not just wear your rubber Donald Trump mask to a crowded theater and flail your octopi limbs at the screen?

When he left Harvard, he threw his cell phone in the Charles, stomped on his MacBook in $365 work boots. Hanging out all day and night at the Food Emporium on East 59th, he's hired by a hedge fund manager to regulate his offsprings' use of screens. The adult daughter (stepsister to the children of her father's third wife and SoulCycle guru) is played by a full-color hologram of Carole Lombard. She visits each evening to dilate the children's eyes to test for Facebook infestation. Always aglow, she's thrilled by the prospect of having a man to boss around. William Powell, perfectly modulated like unsweetened apricot preserves, saves the day so many times, everyone forgets what day it is. Years later, when they are old together and the ocean swallows Manhattan, they are still holding hands, demonstrating the elasticity of proto-apocalyptic feminist marriage.

Dinner began with an aspic shaped like a falling-down bridge and ended with the Mr. and Mrs. tag-teaming the trifle. Discretion frequently hidden in the petals of the petunia lay naked, prone on the dining room table, waiting for the guests to gasp. Was it the cook or the wind catapulting dust through the foyer? Was that thud yesterday's croissants boomeranging the vestibule or the revolution overtaking the streets? Everything smelled like fear, which smelled like a combination of earwax and raspberry vinegar. We curled ourselves inside the curve of a question mark and slept for most of the year. Our dreams resembled the clacking of fingers on a keyboard or the gleam of a souffléed-omelet dawn. The rhythm of our breath in our sleep was the only consolation for the maid. *Their rest is the only relief,* agreed the broom.

When they draw the brocade curtain back to reveal who's secretly singing, the actress in the feather evening gown runs away.

Now exposed, the algorithm keeps crooning.

Tears stream from the stage lights onto the audience.

Does anyone notice the sound of one foot tapping?

The shadow of Gene Kelly's floating face morphing into laughter, then rain?

#XYZBCA

The year a man got famous for eating rotisserie chickens, I learned how to remove glitter nail polish from the bed. In between, my mother died and a friend from elementary school got bit by an ex-boyfriend's new puppy. Things shrunk down. A second moon appeared. If you got close to it, you could smell an oil spill strangling the imprint of what we thought was Earth. I told everyone online about how we placed a blow-up kiddie pool in the middle of the living room, but actually there was no "we." It was just me with my tub filled with flat Diet Coke. I soaked my feet in the dark liquid and watched a trio of monitors hanging from windowless frames. On the first screen: my childhood, the years my calves were bruised from running in shorts through brambles. On the second: the person I never got to be, a woman voguing in the middle of an airfield. *What about the third monitor?* a voice not my own asked. *Can somebody turn it on?*

I was looking up anagrams of my middle name when I heard a scratching from uncategorized bivalves establishing a new species beneath the carpet. Thus began my life as a clam-cognizant, neo-olfactory, intra-confessional, proto-shambolic coordinologist, and ended my career as a poet. I didn't mourn it. I was sitting on my balance ball and throwing pieces of masticated popcorn at the screen when the possibilities of canned air overcame my fear of carnivorous plants. I realized that the shortest distance between the monitor and refrigerator was through the blockchain, and this was one of many revelations that would come to loosen the thread of spittle connecting meaning to matter. Finally, I could hear the thunderous stomping of the child upstairs without missing my toddlerhood, and I didn't mind that my aging torso was replaced with a small, square house. If my eyes were actually windows, I was happy to draw the blinds.

NOT A LIMIT, BUT A FRAME

Days arrive, bundled in down jackets, so we don't notice they are actually years. Birdsongs dig a hole in the rug. The sinuous wedding curtain no longer divides the space between the living and the dead. We are now all officially the in-between: part plug-and-play infant, part magenta-fur lawn chair. When it's time for breakfast, flute music exits the mouth of a somewhat crushed doll. A bridge with missing girders connects the bedroom to the bath, the refrigerator to the gap in my gut. I never thought my eyes would be capable of seeing in so many directions: inward, vertical, perpendicular, onward, and—sometimes—even through.

HOW MANY INTERNETS DOES IT TAKE TO CHANGE A LIGHTBULB?

The young man whose braces once scratched your gums is now old. He lives alone in a city with no buses.

Static replaces your arthritic knee.

The girl whose red hair hypnotized the elementary school is appointed the head of advertising for a company that manufactures tourniquets—or is it knives?

The waterfalls within the cave of your mouth are now error messages.

You wake up each day inside an actual computer and claim it's possible to unplug.

The version of yourself that once haunted dive-bar bathrooms has been sober for 118 years.

A cursor is your blinking eye.

Meanwhile, a woman complains that her ex-husband has married a mannequin, but she's a mannequin too.

In the same ten-by-ten meat locker, two presidents lead two nations. Each speaks a language only one citizen understands.

You compose your manifesto in stick-on eyelashes, stand on the rocking chair to yell at the ceiling fan, but there is no rocking chair.

Years later, the mainframe is inside of you instead of you inside of it.

Your heart beats in binary code. Your finger points everywhere but here.

OUT THE WINDOW, A CAT'S CRY IS A PORTAL TO THE INTERNET OF NEED

A man with a daffodil face pretends to sing opera in the shower.

A woman with a tuba for legs moans for a working socket.

The television opens its mouth and another television falls out.

The two sides of my headphones split apart: the left moves to Florida, the right takes up residence on the moon.

Before long, I am screaming so loud that the dogs in China eat each other's bones and brains and shit out 1,034 miniature plastic dogs.

My skin curls itself around the digital clock.

My eyes switch places with each other.

Everyone I ever knew hides their wallet in my sofa and their cash in the dying spider plant.

The picture of a cat in heat falls off the wall and turns into a living beast.

Under the bookshelf, the mice play hospital. We pretend the sound of their lovemaking is an ambulance on the way.

IN MY PAST LIFE I WAS ONLY 57½% DATA

When we woke up to the vampire yelling on TV, we thought the flag in his hand would one day turn into a rose.

You said, "Just because there's a rupture in the space-time continuum doesn't mean all language is just wrapping paper designed to conceal a bored god's lump of gruel."

I said nothing but kept ripping off the wallpaper until the ceiling started to bleed.

I was certain that the ghost chasing me through the half-open window was just a bedsheet with my own anger inside.

A year later, I was the blank square at the center of a hashtag, and you were a screaming-mouth meme retweeted into the void.

I wanted to just accept it—to be able to open myself—to touch with each finger—the newly reconstituted world.

You've memorized all the words that rhyme with cacophony, but still you can't revise the writing on the wallflower.

That's capitalism, my friend, decked out again in a gold mankini, big toe stuck trapezoidally in another country's cottage fries.

Hold still and let the twentieth century sink in beside you.

Check a box if:

- ☐ (A) The weather portends the possibility of soup.
- ☐ (B) All the charm wore off when they put the river in a tourniquet.
- ☐ (C) To say "The lioness is in waiting" is just another way of saying you've lost.
- ☐ (D) All or none of the above.

THE FUTURE IS A BATHTUB FILLED WITH PURE RAGE

After the warnings are subtweeted as jokes // after the quizzes shrivel up // after the factory rips off its wings // after a multiverse is found in a Barbie's missing asshole // after I wake up to an ocean on fire // after I unplug the moment // after you soak up the sound // absorb the fear in the petunia // after we sweep up the squawking // rejigger the excess // after the wedding of misanthropes and mist // after the yelling rehearsal // after we fall out of bed // after the truth bomb is unbombed // after you right-click the callout // after you uninstall the update // after I left-click the catastrophe // unpack the paranormal // after the pause before the yell // after the lavender-scented tremors and the sound of something not wind

only then can we be part-god/part-meme, only then can we navigate the soft spots we desire, only then can we unzip the narrative—friend–enemy–follower–wizened pronouncer–dust influencer–baby ghost, just wait—one day we'll float above the neighbor's clickety-clack, smash language against tundra into smoke

Strangers ask how you feel about terror, but when you hear *Tell her* you wonder, *Who is this "her" and why is she getting all the attention?* This is a problem with coalition building. You think you are holding hands with another, but it's actually an empty rubber glove. De Chirico was right about *The Song of Love*. Cruelty makes more sense when you are looking at an empty piazza than a bustling square. In the algorithmic state, the town square is a cage where we think we are having sex until we wake up and find we are thumb wrestling a robot ghost. Understand, I didn't grow up in this pixelscape. I don't know how to remake my face into the face one recognizes in the mirror. Do you still remember how it felt to share a boysenberry milkshake in the back of a truck? Have you ever felt real seafoam on another person's thinning hair? You know I was a person once with actual wet boots. Back then, I only gurgled like protodata when it rained.

THE WAY THE DATA CRUMBLES

There was never an algorithmic sex act. That wasn't a real breast that flashed like Magritte's pipe on your tongue. There is no smell of menstrual blood. Still, despite the billions of Barbie dolls clogging the ocean, fish attempt to breathe and fall in love. Seahorses organize the territory.

When I still believed in the possibility of a future on earth, I walked along the shore, collecting letters in bottles. One was written in microscript and purported to tell the history of slavery through the allegory of the cave. The others you had to lick to understand.

THE HAUNTED HOUSEPLANT

We spend the night wondering if the murmured-to cantaloupes will be able to ride their winged chariots again. Will the celestial guillotines awaken? Can the ass of the past sprout fangs? Or at least teeth?

When will my computer open its eyes? Will my hard drive rip off its database and reveal its washboard abs? How will we replace the search engine with energetic moss? Can we finally rip away the monitor's gold-plated strap-on?

I pretend sometimes that I know we will be happy again, able to lick the sludge off our lips, to chomp on pearly apples whose crunchy authenticity will erase the moonscapes we lost. Sometimes I am able to conjure up the beauty of this pause—can glimpse the cat's whiskers conducting the star's silent music.

Can you see it too? Can you feel it blowing through the thin hairs on your limbs?

NO ONE COULD FORGET THE
UPROARIOUS LAUGHTER

Where do the doctors go when the x-ray convention gets canceled? What sort of ice machine keeps the water constantly moving? What monster fits best in a fur purse? Why don't trees fall apart when you cry? What's the opposite of a scar? Why undo a why?

What could have been a future in mountaineering was just a remote control in lederhosen. What could have been an answer to a question was instead a series of questions, each progressively smaller in size, as if they'd been arranged by a god with a too-refined sense of humor.

"Like Santa Claus with a cold," you said dismissively.

By Tuesday morning, all language started to sound like a secret shared through a pixie cup on a string. Despite the sideways look I gave the bartender, I preferred life this way. It kept the brain-sized mushroom clouds in check.

COORDINATES

After a life in poetry, there is always an office chair, a stack of celebrity magazines, and a broken paper shredder.

Love itself becomes the fifth dimension.

Tough pancakes, says the bridge gnome, by which he means, "It's time to reboot the soundtrack, time to rupture your equipment cloud and extol the dust."

In a previous life, you found a rowboat trapped in the middle of a lake. A fish entered your skin and you convinced yourself you were half trout, half cloud, part of a long line of aquatic gods sent to the surface to explain the importance of loss.

After you failed, the pink around the edges of language blurred the pain.

You dug a hole into the center, swaddled it in swamp grass—buried it far from the fossilized moss.

TIKKUN OLAM

When I was a child, we said, "Next year in Jerusalem," and we meant not the international city, heart of three religions, but the other, less tactile, city, the center of the proto-internet, city of starlight and Talmudic honeycombs. When my sister said "Israel" she meant a sky-blue room where the letters of the Torah glowed like a string of bloody hearts. When I said it, I meant a kibbutz where I might have multiple orgasms, write poetry, and farm radishes. I longed for the basement rooms where my ancestors ate knishes while debating the meaning of Marx. When we imagined freeing the slaves, we meant not just the Jewish slaves. We fantasized about traveling simultaneously backward and forward in time, unknotting the lynch knots from pixelated, dehistoricized trees.

MY COUNTRY HAS TURNED INTO A
HAUNTED HOUSE

Even if you put a white sheet over your brain, you can't scare the future out of her werewolf suit.

The crowd that waits to enter is losing patience with quality control; they want new sneakers to walk them into static.

This is how narrative works. The arrow that exits your heart used to be a needle sewing the present to the past, but now it just points to itself. So what? What kind of why?

The taste of sulfur wakes you up and you find yourself at the corner of Hot Pants and Rage holding a sign to protest an identity that hasn't been invented yet.

Did you think a different sort of magic was possible?

Come closer to smell the history drying on your skin. It looks like talcum powder, but no matter how much you wiggle your limbs and dance, it never shakes off.

MY SORROW IS A BILLBOARD PAINTED
WITH CLOUDS

When the mass shootings are broadcast live, the internet screams, *Look, my tears are made of Beanie Baby frogs, tears of baby seals clubbed with incel memes, tears of premasticated marshmallows, of popcorn chicken refusing to pop, of robot porcupines strutting to their jobs at the baby factory or hobnobbing with RIP flies!* I try to believe this sorrow. In my room at night, I draw pictures of the internet: (1) the internet as a sunglasses-wearing movie star hugging us all; (2) the internet as a house-sized cello played by a bow; (3) the internet as a movie whose subtitles are replaced by a transcript of eavesdropped chatter. In bed, I see the internet as a boat large enough to hold us all. On the moon, we feel each other's lungs with only our fingertips. *Look*, I say, *here is the open mouth of the galaxy, and there we are inside it: typing or tapping or swiping away.* In the morning when I wake, I realize I myself am the internet. I glance in the mirror and my face is an amalgam of every demographic, a map with cities crashing into each other like bumper cars, data nose-diving like private planes.

HOW TO CHANGE THE FILTER ON THE
DEVELOPING CELL MATTER IN YOUR WOMB

If you wake up early, the genre is rom-com: the cells trade insults with a grad-student waitress with dimples.

If you microwave your frozen Pop-Tart, it's sci-fi. An alien beams up a fertilized egg so they can kibbitz about time travel.

If you double the shots in your Americano: action! A fetus drives a McLaren 720S into an amniotic sac.

If you choose to go back to bed—maybe mumblecore? You keep adjusting the womb's speaker, but still—you can't make out . . .

If you read the *New York Times* on your cell phone, it's clearly an Oscar winner. The sibling of the disabled fetus learns how to hide his tears at the truck-stop cervix.

If you read the back of the cereal box, it's a documentary. A talking head explains why the fetus isn't kicking.

If you throw the cereal box against the wall: French New Wave. The fetus's naked ass complicates the meta-dialogue about the commercialization of Hollywood film.

If you wear red lipstick under your KN95, a musical is born. In glittery feathers, the mother's bladder tap-dances. The thin hairs on the fetus sway together Busby Berkeley–style, forming an arch, then spiraling into numerous rhinestone-adorned spokes.

If you cry in the driver's seat of your minivan: melodrama strikes! Once the fetus falls in love, his deadly illness is detected.

If you text your ex an inscrutable emoji—oh, the horror: the fetus attacks the host with dissonant chords.

If you take a selfie with your childhood stuffie: Studio Ghibli. The fetus morphs into a cat-shaped balloon and floats out of the womb.

If you walk to work, it's a costume drama. Each style of chapeau suggests a new stage in the fetus's psychological development.

If you skip work, it's film noir. It was all the dame's scheme. There never was a fetus in the womb.

PREQUEL

The evening your torso becomes a TV tuned to Fox News, your memories are replaced with a laugh track. The space between then and now grows porous, comes to resemble the underside of an overused yellow sponge. Before you can say what you think, your son has turned into a giraffe. He trims the hedges with his metal tongue. While one daughter cuts the plugs off all the appliances, dressing them up as if they were glamorous dolls, your other daughter refuses to converse. Her silence is a black box sinking imperceptibly into the living room floor. When your wife's polyester nightie starts a fire, your mother-in-law's voice echoes like an opera through the blaze. You demand that the windows are swapped for pictures of ghosts, that your name is engraved on the largest flame. The sinks overflow with canola oil, then beer. The more you yell, the harder it is for anyone to hear.

A songbird's idea of refusal quavered, gunking up reality with music. The sky adieu-ed the end times with memories of future blood. *My appetites or yours, hon?* said no one to nothing.

Misled by lopsided horse clouds, the window was declared the new expanse. Office parties smelling of last century drifted in and dispersed. Life became a series of toes recalibrating the atmosphere through boredom and smoke.

Still, fear battered the dust mites awake. What used to be my country raptured the horizon's teeth—ecstatic options sprinkling emotions in the mix, hastening the return of reality as 89.3 percent dream.

TAXONOMY

Despite the apocalyptic matterscape, knives slice open the quandary. Tough. Tufted. A thumb-sized cave with god-sized stalagmites quivering inside.

Here becomes I becomes we.

The color of eye whites at midnight. The underside of a knee.

Does this mean we are immune to the seduction of sunlight on a patio table—free from the starlight's hagiography? The cell phone's quacking ring?

THE FUTURE LEAKS INTO THE PAST

Some days I would push my chair to the window and get angry when no one could tell that I was also a window.

Other days I'd find the window in my heart. I'd open it so all the swallows could fly out, breaking everything not amenable to the possibility of loss.

I met a few species of creatures I would be capable of loving, but more often I failed.

One day, the computer opened its mouth and swallowed the past, so all that was left of the present was a silent movie hidden behind a velvet curtain.

Only the mice found holes in the narrative and could make a sort of home there.

The rest of us just complained about the end.

EVERYTHING OUTSIDE IS SOMEONE'S INSIDE

With knitting needles and dental floss, we invented what would come to be called the internet.

Wallpapered. Dusty. The color of nectarine breath. The smell of a mop.

Later, when we shut the lights off and slipped into our cell phone's cushion, we dreamt of a different future, one where we could wear our organs on our outside, where our small intestines could jangle so our employers would understand, and sympathize.

In our sleep, we crawled farther inside, deeper into the computer's bloody organs.

There, we found the button that would turn history back.

I sucked on it until something resembling milk dripped out.

DATA MIND

The joke that replaced our democracy kept waiting for the laugh track to return. I tried to recalibrate my response, tried to say "No, thank you" without turning off the lights. What misery was left I swept up, hid away in a cracked jar. I cried out, *Please bring me your cheese fries longing to be free.*

I tried again. I chanted, *Now.* I called out, *When.*

All the clocks in the underground supermarket struck the same mistake twice. The clown shoes grew a city on their nose. The locks picked themselves. The radio swallowed the television, which swallowed an old hunk of cheese.

What I thought was my childhood wore a Groucho Marx mustache on her chest.

The joke tap-danced on the wall. The wall tap-danced on the joke.

I clapped my hands together as hard as I could, but I couldn't make anything stop.

ACKNOWLEDGMENTS

My thanks to the editors of the following publications, in which versions of these poems previously appeared, sometimes under slightly different titles:

Boog City: "The Algorithm Ate My Lunch," "*Dinner at Eight*," "*My Man Godfrey* for the Internet Age," and "The Way the Data Crumbles"

The Brooklyn Rail: "The Future Is a Bathtub Filled with Pure Rage" and "The Future Leaks into the Past"

Concision Poetry Journal: "Data Mind," "Me Day!," "My American Name Is Money," and "Taxonomy"

Cruel Garters: "Prequel"

Denver Quarterly: "This Cat Video Will Change Your Life"

Digital Vestiges: "The Haunted Houseplant," "How Many Internets Does It Take to Change a Lightbulb?," "No One Could Forget the Uproarious Laughter," "Out the Window, a Cat's Cry Is a Portal to the Internet of Need," and "Your Ick Is My Yum"

Explorations in Media Ecology: "The Early Adopter" (as "The Early Adaptor"), "It's Not a Language If Everyone Understands It" (as "It's Still a Language If No One Understands It"), and the memes [The Future Leaks into the Past], [If My Eyes Are Actually Windows, I'm Happy to Draw the Blinds], [It's Still a Language If No One Understands It], and [Language Is Always Both Tenor and Vehicle]

Georgia Review: "ChapStick Traces," "How to Change the Filter on the Developing Cell Matter in Your Womb," and "My Sorrow Is a Billboard Painted with Clouds"

The Glacier: "Did You Know That Your Doppelgänger Is Licking Chaos on the Dark Web?," "How It Started / How It's Going," *"Singin' in the Rain,"* and "You Won't Believe How Your Favorite Childhood Star Looks Now"

Journal of NJ Poets: "The Internet Is Not the City" and "The Least Witchy Witch on the Internet"

The Laurel Review: "Does This Data Make Me Look Fat?," "A Heart Is Not a Metaphor," and "Outrage Fatigue"

Limp Wrist: "Barbie Attempts to Gain Control of the Algorithmic State"

Maintenant 15: "The Year the Internet Was a Glitching Map"

Marsh Hawk Review: "Poetica Fondant"

New American Writing: *"The Matrix,"* "My Breast Squirts Milk at the Algorithmic State" and "My Country Has Turned into a Haunted House"

Pangyrus: "Photographing Your Salad Turns It into a Ghost"

Pithead Chapel: *"Something Wild"*

Posit: "In *The Matrix* Starring Nicolas Cage"

The Rumpus: "Are You the Invisible Song That Was Playing?," "Barbie Attempts to Gain Control of the Algorithmic State," "The Future Leaks into the Past," and "Tikkun Olam"

Tribes: "These Six Emojis Explain Your Life Right Now" and *"The Warriors"*

Unbroken: "Dataverse" and "#xyzbca"

Volt Journal: "My American Name Is Money"

"The Algorithm Ate My Lunch," "My American Name Is Money," "In *The Matrix* Starring Nicolas Cage," and "*The Matrix*" were reprinted in *Contemporary Surrealist and Magical Realist Poetry: An International Anthology*, ed. Jonas Zdanys (Lamar University Literary Press, 2022).

I am indebted to friends who gave me feedback on this work in development: Martine Bellen, Boni Joi, Sharon Mesmer, Jean-Paul Pecqueur, Rick Snyder, and Yerra Sugarman, as well as Elaine Equi, who encouraged me to send work out to more journals and whose work and friendship always inspire me. Also, Douglas Rothschild, who helped me with the title of "Poetica Fondant." In addition, I want to thank my friends who read drafts of this manuscript and offered encouragement: Charles Borkhuis, Paula Cisewski, Jordan Davis, Caroline Hagood, and Chris Stroffolino. And to Lucy Biederman, for her contribution to the process. I am especially grateful to my husband, Bob, who is usually my first reader.

Also, thank you to the editors of Hanging Loose Press for publishing my work since I was a child and for welcoming me to the other side of the publishing table, and to everyone at Rutgers for letting me teach what I love, especially Carolyn Williams.

Working with Northwestern University Press has been wonderful. Thank you to Anne Gendler, Charlotte Keathley, Mary Klein, Maddie Schultz, Lauren Smith, and especially Marisa Siegel. As a lover of poetry in translation, I am honored to have this book under the Curbstone imprint.

NOTE

The titles of the poems "My Country Has Turned into a Haunted House," "My American Name Is Money," and "Photographing Your Salad Turns It into a Ghost" are taken from collaged artworks by Simon Evans and Sarah Lannan (collectively known as Simon Evans™). I fell in love with the lines when I saw them at a show in the spring of 2019 at the James Cohan Gallery.